24.95

D1105778

Distributed by
**BEEKMAN PUBLISHERS, INC.**
P.O. Box 888
Woodstock, NY 12498-0888 USA
(914) 679-2300 • (888) BEEKMAN

# OLD INVERNESS IN PICTURES

# OLD INVERNESS IN PICTURES

*Published by*

PAUL HARRIS PUBLISHING

*in association with*

INVERNESS FIELD CLUB

*First published 1978 by*
*Paul Harris Publishing*
*25 London Street, Edinburgh*
*in association with Inverness Field Club*
*© Copyright Inverness Field Club 1978*

ISBN 0 904505 50 2

*Printed by*
*John G Eccles Printers Ltd, Inverness*

# ACKNOWLEDGMENTS

"There are many people to whom whatever is old is uninteresting," wrote Miss Anderson in 1885 in *Inverness before the Railways* and *Old Inverness in Pictures* is not for them. It is rather, to quote her further, for those other "persons to whom the streets of Inverness are haunted by forms unseen by other eyes, and who, notwithstanding the extension and improvements of the town, think with regret of the old country walks once so rural and retired, but now built over, and of the old buildings now pulled down to make way for modern ones, or turned to uses very different from those originally intended."

When the Inverness Field Club published *The Hub of the Highlands; the Book of Inverness and District* in 1975 to mark its Centenary, much was written about the Royal Burgh, but the illustrations were necessarily spread over the whole range of subjects covered by the various articles. To remedy this, the Field Club now offers this collection of scenes of Inverness, its buildings, people, games, industries and occasions from 1842 until the 1970s.

To those who have allowed us to make use of pictures from their own collections, to the Museum and Art Gallery, whose growing files were opened freely for selection, to the Inverness, Loch Ness and Nairn Tourist Association for their generous offer in a time of financial stringency, to the Highlands and Islands Development Board for a Working Capital Loan the thanks of the Field Club must be paid. Nor must those be forgotten who, whether members or not, subscribed and whose names will be found at the end of this book, those who have since ordered copies, those whose pictures were not used in the final selection, and all those that we hope will buy and enjoy this book. Without the co-operation of everyone mentioned in this paragraph, and others as well, this book would never have appeared.

The following have kindly allowed us to use their pictures and, if any copyright has been infringed, we hope to be forgiven.

Mr W. Balfour, Inverness, 129, 130.
Miss Barron, The Inverness Courier, 9, 84, 85, 136, 163, 169, 199, 211.
Bingham, Hughes & Macpherson, Inverness, 210.
Mr A. Cadenhead, Raigmore, 87.
Mr J. Campbell, Island Bank Road, 7, 10, 22, 62, 66, 69, 173, 193.
Mr J.W. Campbell, Darris Road, 206, 207, 208.
Mrs Chisholm, Culloden, 198.
Mrs Clark, Drumblair Crescent, 141, 142, 143.
Miss Dallas, Kingsmills Road, 100, 103, 137, 153, 155, 159, 160, 174, 175, 187, 189, 215.
Mr J. England Kerr, Ladies Walk, 107, 108.
Mr A. Fleming, Inverness, 29, 102, 167, 168, 209.
Fraser and McColl, Eastgate, 203.
Mrs Fresson, Merlewood Road, 121, 122, 126, 194, 195.
Mr W. Glashan, Glenburn Drive, 25, 27, 41, 67.

Loraine Maclean of Dochgarroch,<br>
Editor.

June, 1978

# THE BACKGROUND TO THE PICTURES

It is fitting, I think, to recall Dr D.J. MacDonald's final sentence from his paper 'Life in Old Inverness' in Inverness Field Club's Centenary Volume *The Hub of the Highlands*. His words, that 'some aspects of Life in Old Inverness are worthy of being hung as pictures of living interest even today', have in a sense inspired this book of photographs of Inverness and its folk during the last century or so.

As we look back from the last quarter of the 20th century to the events, personalities and environment of Old Inverness and round about, as seen through the eye of the camera, we can be grateful that so many photographs, professional and amateur, of Victorian and later times, have preserved for us visual evidence of the atmosphere and essence of a way of life that has quite changed. A hundred years and more ago, life undoubtedly moved at a slower pace, and in a quieter and less polluted environment. While we cannot, from pictures, fully appreciate the thoughts that were in people's minds, or how exactly they expressed themselves in words, the development of the camera has given us a fascinating insight into the lives and activities of our grandparents and great-grandparents. This recording of events by the camera allows us something our great-grandparents could not experience — the facility not only to savour scenes from the past, but also to study accurate pictorial representations more true to life than the products of the artist's brush, however realistic.

Inverness was a smaller town in the mid-nineteenth century, with just a third of the present population, and its area was limited, so that almost everyone knew everyone else. Around 1850 the life-style of the Invernessian and the Highlander was changing from the old order, and the camera became the recorder of these historic changes.

Whereas the Battle of Culloden in 1746 signified the end of an era and the last chapter of the old Highland way of life, the year 1855 could be regarded as the real beginning of the modern Highlands. When Fort George was completed by General Skinner in 1769, it cost £160,000 and was quite the largest project ever to have been constructed in Northern Scotland: then in 1822 the Caledonian Canal, engineered by Thomas Telford, at a cost of just over £900,000, was opened. But Fort George and the canal had little significant effect on modern Highland history: the Fort, despite its magnificent military engineering, never experienced warfare, while the Canal, for all its convenient and scenic route from east to west, has never been a financial success. When in 1855 Joseph Mitchell the Inverness engineer, completed the Inverness to Nairn railway, he initiated the great movement and drive that took the 'Capital of the Highlands' into the thriving Victorian world of economics and industrial progress. After the failure of the Jacobite cause and the end of the clan system with its subsistence-level pastoral/agricultural economy, Inverness had suffered a great decline in trade and prosperity. Even after 1800 when Telford improved and extended the military road network, land communications were tenuous between North Scotland and the more populous, industrial regions of the South. Inverness was therefore an outpost town in the Highlands, a centre for trading in the North only, and, by 1850, had but slowly recovered in status and prosperity, gradually spreading west of the river beyond the old mediaeval nucleus. Increase in population was due to its attraction for Highland folk, driven from the straths and glens by the unhappy Clearances. Although never a 'Gaelic' town, this important influx of Gaels is epitomised by the Highland surnames of ten out of thirteen Provosts between 1800 and 1850.

Inverness has been rightly called a Railway-Age town — the construction of the railway to Nairn in 1855, followed by other lines radiating north, west and south from the Highland Capital, initiated a great expansion of commercial development and an era of new building during the latter half of the 19th century into Edwardian times. The old stone Ness Bridge, swept away by the 1849 spate, was replaced by the elegant Suspension Bridge in 1855, by which date many of the town's important public buildings had been erected: the new Castle and Courthouse, the Steeple, the Infirmary, the Northern Meetings Rooms, the Caledonian Bank (now Bank of Scotland), Farraline Park Institution, the old Academy, the Roman Catholic Chapel, and the West Church. More streets were laid out about 1860, including Union Street (from Station Square to Church Street), and, west of the river, Ardross Street and Terrace, and Tomnahurich Street. New houses, indeed mansions, were erected on the Hill, between Castle Street and Petty Street (now Eastgate), and between Kingsmills Road and the river-side.

Many of the handsome churches of the Victorians still contribute to the architectural quality of our riverside skyline, despite the sterile designs of adjacent office development blocks built in our own times. The temples of God even today excel those of Mammon.

Dr Alexander Ross, the architect — he was Provost of Inverness from 1889-95 — designed several beautiful town churches; the Cathedral of St Andrew (1866-9), St Columba High and the Free North Churches, and the Tweedmouth Chapel at the Infirmary. Other fine churches are Queen Street Church (architect — Pond Macdonald), St Stephen's Church (architect — W.L. Carruthers). The Episcopalian Church of St Michael and All Angels has a splendid interior designed by the famous ecclesiastical architect Sir Ninian Comper.

Inverness has been fortunate in that twice during the last century an excellent pictorial record has been made of the historic buildings under threat or demolished. In 1903 Robert Carruthers and Sons published a series of fine prints by Pierre Delavault, art master at Inverness Royal Academy. More recently, another incomer, William Glashan, the architect, has recorded with pen and brush the buildings and streets which vanished in the 1960s and 70s — many of his pictures are on view in the Inverness Museum.

Good examples of Victorian and Edwardian architecture are the flamboyantly-turreted Town House (1878), Ardkeen Tower (1842-5), the Royal Academy (1895), and Dr Ross's two hotels west of the river, the Palace and the Columba. Ross would seem to have been the master-mind behind the planning and layout of corridor streets like Queensgate, and of the pedestrian-only Market Arcade, a covered shopping precinct of considerable architectural and spatial quality.

But good building and sensitive planning in Inverness ended after the first decade of the twentieth century. Following the First World War there was a lowering of standards. The change came with the adoption of cheap and nasty 'jerry-building', and both public authority and private developments reflected lack of architectural character and loss of sense of good-mannered townscape, due partly to shortage of finance but largely to paucity of imaginative design. The Invernessian-in-the-street's impression, rightly or wrongly, is that architecture and planning have, since the Second World War, combined to produce buildings of outstanding ugliness and lack of elegance in their exterior aspects, although, paradoxically, present-day interior design and planning is generally far more imaginative than that of last century's architects. In this town, despite recent demolitions of buildings of recognised architectural and historical merit such as Queen Mary's House (early 16th century), Raining's School (1757), Bught House (18th century), Fraser of Bunchrew's House (late 18th century), Provost Mackintosh's House (c. 1800), Raigmore House (c. 1840), Queensgate Post Office (1888), and others, there are now hopeful signs of a return to the higher architectural standards of the past. First-class rehabilitation and expert conservation work has ensured the survival of Abertarff's House (1597); Dunbar's Hospital (1668) — restoration architect: Alexander Cullen; Bow Court (1729) — restoration architect: William Glashan: Church Gate Cottage (c. 1770); while important public buildings such as the Castle, the Town House and the Steeple have been enhanced by a face-lift with stone-cleaning. So some buildings of the past will have a future, and architecture may again become an art instead of a 'system'.

I ponder on the possibility of restoration work being executed in the year 2078 on the office-development-boxes of today. It seems more probable that, like the multi-storey flats already being demolished after a decade or so, the so-called 'international-style' buildings of the brutalist movement will prove uneconomic, and will not survive into the 21st century.

The Victorian age produced great engineers and it is recognised that, after Telford, one of the most able was Joseph Mitchell of Inverness. He epitomised the local spirit of enterprise in that, instead of waiting for the railways to reach the Highlands from the south, he persuaded Invernessians to promote their own town to be the railway centre of Northern Scotland. Of course, the town owed its original foundation to its geographical situation as a nodal point of overland and sea and freshwater routes. But earlier means of communication, on foot, on horse, coach or boat, were all slow-paced compared to the railways, which for the first time, brought Inverness within speedy reach of the rest of Scotland, and launched a new era of trade, industry and prosperity.

Soon the new railways severely affected the waterborne traffic along the Caledonian Canal, and also the stage-coaches travelling along the dusty Parliamentary roads. At intervals along these roads, after the 1823 Toll Gate Act, gates and toll-houses were erected, usually on the outskirts of towns and villages. Tolls were collected to finance road maintenance; always unpopular, they were abolished in 1878. The toll-houses continued as private dwellings, of the three situated at the approaches to Inverness, only that between Muirtown Canal Bridge and Clachnaharry village survives today. Drakies Tollhouse stood near where the entrance to Raigmore New

Central Hospital is now, while the sad ruin of Stoneyfield Tollhouse is a tribute to the complete lack of care by the local authority who acquired it in 1969 when the Nairn road was re-aligned. How does it come about that acquisition by a public authority, authorised as the caretaker and guardian of our architectural heritage, so often becomes a 'kiss of death'?

After 1855, railway fever gripped Invernessians and the Highlands, just as it raged unabated further south. From the Lochgorm Locomotive Works, built in 1864, came many grand old long-chimneyed steam engines, with local names like 'Raigmore', 'Clachnacuddin', 'Rosehaugh', and 'Strathpeffer'. These and other powerful and distinctive steam locomotives were designed by David Jones, born in Manchester of Welsh ancestry, Superintendent at Lochgorm between 1870 and 1896.

Joseph Mitchell's dream was of a rail link from Inverness to Perth by the Druimuachdar Pass but, although the Inverness and Perth Railway Company was formed in 1844, the scheme was not accepted by Parliament. After 1855 Mitchell's railway schemes were backed financially by Sir Alexander Matheson of Ardross, M.P. for Inverness, a landed proprietor who used his fortunes and know-how to benefit the Highlands. By 1858 the eastward line towards Aberdeen had linked up with the Great North of Scotland Railway at Keith. Mitchell's dream — the line to Perth — was eventually realised with the opening of the railroad over the Grampians by Forres, Dava and Strathspey in 1863.

Inverness was the headquarters of the Highland Railway until 1923, when the company was merged into the London Midland and Scottish Railway. The Highland was one of the most fascinating of the old railway companies and the town provided most of its work-force. In the hundred years after 1855, during which rail travel was the best and cheapest, the line had a character of its own, being particularly noted for its attractive green Inverness-built locomotives.

Despite the invention of the internal combustion engine in the 1880s it was not until the First World War that the automobile became a frequent vehicle in the town. Macrae and Dick's horse cabs continued until the mid-twenties. Only after the Second World War did the private motor car become a more convenient and less expensive form of transport, particularly for the family. About the same time Highland Omnibuses served the town as public transport. Today, however, the long-term future of the motorised vehicle may be seriously affected if the advantages become outweighed by serious and increasing disadvantages, such as rising petrol costs, mammoth-juggernauts on roads, and pollution from exhausts in our streets.

Meanwhile, like the railway enthusiasts' fanaticism for vintage steam locomotives and trains, so we have the present paradoxical interest in motoring of the past, with veteran car owners in Inverness enjoying a jaunt along tarmac raods, the gentlemen in caps and goggles, the ladies with heads enscarved — a breath of those Edwardian days when highways were dusty, speed was leisurely, and the automobile was a novelty.

Like the railways, air transport in North Scotland started in Inverness. Captain E.E. Fresson was an Englishman who pioneered civil aviation throughout the Highlands and Islands from his base at Longman Municipal Aerodrome, where he operated long before Dalcross became Inverness Airport. The first flight in the Highland Airways service to Wick and Orkney took off on 8th May, 1933, and this was extended to link up with Aberdeen, and then with Shetland, and eventually also with Stornoway. Highland Airways, in 1935, joined with United Airways, working with Northern and Scottish Airways, Renfrew, and Inverness then had an air-service south to Glasgow. By 1937 these Highland and Scottish companies became part of British Airways with connecting flights to Europe. Fresson, like Telford and Mitchell, has become a legendary name in the development of transport in the North. He and his pilots flew De Havilland Rapide aeroplanes after 1935, and this involved the building of larger hangars, one or two of which still stand among the buildings of the Longman Industrial Estate. Conditions in the 1930s were much more primitive than now: Captain Fresson and his daring young men in their flying machines took off from bumpy grass runways — at first with no radio contacts or other air-navigational aids — and flew through storms and fogs, and over high mountains and rough waters, plus enemy action in the Second World War, to land passengers and mail safely on little pocket-handkerchiefs of airfields in the north and the islands.

Before the coming of rail and air travel, the town derived much of its trade and commerce by means of its harbour at the mouth of the Ness. About 1850 the Inverness Harbour Trust, consisting of seventeen councillors, five merchants, and five shipowners, controlled the port, and guided by Joseph Mitchell as engineer, their scheme of modernisation gave the harbour its present layout. Until the advent of railways, the port was a busy place dealing with both passengers and goods. Like the stage-coaches of the first half of the 19th century, the wooden sailing ships also rejoiced in grand old romantic names, such as the *North Star,* sailing from Thornbush Quay to London every second Monday, taking 63 hours: fares were £4 (cabin) and £2:12:6, in the pre-decimal coinage, for steerage accommodation. Then there were the *Maid of Morven* and the *Duke of Richmond.* In the 1860s Inverness had 216 vessels of over 11,000 registered tonnage. In the 1880s there were further improvements to Shore Street quay, allowing large coal boats to berth: the port became the centre of the coal trade, importing 46,700 tons in 1909.

Shipbuilding was an important industry, as long as ships were wooden, and there were yards on both sides of the river until the 1870s. On the Merkinch side, beside the railway bridge, was Munro's shipyard, near the Thornbush slipway was Macgregor's, where the last schooner to be built was the *Sovereign* in 1878. On the Shore Street side, John Cook's yard occupied the site of the present sawmills, and there were two large yards within 'Cromwell's Fort'. Associated with shipbuilding went sailmaking and ropemaking. The two sailmaking factories were Grant's in the Fort, and Anderson's Thornbush Hemp Manufactory near the Quay; the Ropeworks were in Rose Street.

Throughout the 19th century Inverness increased in importance as an agricultural centre, especially after the establishment of a Sheep and Wool Fair in 1817, the same year in which the *Inverness Courier* was founded in opposition to the *Inverness Journal* established in 1807. The *Journal* lasted for almost half a century, but the *Courier* is now over 160 years old and still going strong, an independent local newspaper of character, and very much an integral part of the Invernessian scene. The same independence of spirit and confidence in Inverness and the Highlands instigated, with local finance, the establishment in 1838 of the Caledonian Banking

Company, which gave beneficial aid to agriculture and trade in the North. This bank survived the economic depression following the failure of the City of Glasgow Bank, and it continued to be independent until 1907, when it amalgamated with the Bank of Scotland, High Street.

By 1850 there were several industries in the town, including the woollen mills at Holm, maltings, of which there were many in the 18th century, three iron foundries, which merged by 1895 into the Rose Street Foundry and Engineering Company Limited, whisky-distilling (three distilleries still exist today), tanning works — the last tannery, Chisholm's, in Gilbert Street, was demolished in 1966 and three breweries — the Thornbush Brewery and Buchanan's Haugh Brewery ceased operating before 1914. Although steam had become the source of power, windmills still existed in the last century, the large one at Thornbush having been built by William Wright in 1827, disused by the 1880s, it was demolished in 1943. The other windmill at the Shore was converted into a clock tower, marking the site of the Cromwellian Fort, its surroundings completely covered over by an unsightly layout of oil-tanks, symbols of today's (and possibly, tomorrow's) energy for commerce and industry.

Adjoining the railway station and marshalling yards the town's first industrial zone was planned and laid out in a rectilinear grid pattern of cobbled streets in the area north of Eastgate. The warehouses and stores of First, Second, Third and Fourth Streets (all demolished in the early 1970s, the site becoming a vast car park) were built to deal with the railhead's goods traffic and wholesale businesses.

In 1870 Mr McGruther and Mr Marshall started their firm which has acted for over a century as merchants for coal, lime and building materials, now developing as suppliers to North Sea oil-firms. It was in 1878 that Roderick Macrae of Beauly and William Dick of Redcastle became partners in a firm offering transport services — 'Landaus, Waggonettes, Phaetons, Dog Carts and Gigs'. A hundred years on, Macrae and Dick is one of the leading motor industry firms in the North of Scotland.

By the end of last century, Inverness was the largest and most important commercial centre north of Aberdeen. The town's businesses then were still fairly self-sufficient, its many independent and successful enterprises being financed without the help of outside capital. Before the First World War, many owner-operated and prosperous commercial premises had been established in the town, to serve the townspeople and the sporting estates and tourists arriving by rail. The bustling invasion of Inverness capes, deerstalker hats, knickerbockers, guns and rods can be visualised as the shooting and fishing seasons started.

In these times horse-drawn gigs and carts clattered over the stone setts of the narrow streets; and, as evening came, shops stayed open much later than now, the small-paned windows gleaming in the gaslight. The compact shopping centre was the heart of the town. Most shops were personally supervised by the shopkeepers and their families, giving individual attention to the public. Where shoppers now pass by the multiples (typical of any town anywhere), they cannot fail to notice that yet another family-owned shop has become an insurance company or building society office, but how many remember the older local establishments such as Mackay's Clan Tartan Warehouse at Castle Street corner, Noble's (later Mackay's)

Bookshop in High Street, Fraser, Ferguson and MacBean, jewellers, Union Street corner, Macleay's the Taxidermists, Jack's the Grocers at the Exchange, Mackintosh and Macleod, the Wine Shop in Queen Mary's House, John MacKenzie 'Caberfeidh', the Bootmakers, Church Street, Alexander Munro's Cycle Depot, and others? And do they ruefully reflect on prices as they were around 1910? — for example, tea at 2/- per lb.; woollen cardigans at 21/6; ladies' blouses — 3/6 and 5/11; whisky at 4/- per bottle; while hotel charges were 2/6 (single bedroom) and 4/- (double bedroom), with lunch at 1/6. We can contrast all that with present-day high inflationary costs and the inevitable trend to establish more impersonal self-service supermarket stores on the outskirts of town, or even further afield.

Through the camera's eye we see the folk of our town at work and play a hundred years back: their social activities and their amusements have been recorded in newspaper reports and elsewhere. How different then were the fashions in dress. Would the crinolined lady or tartan-shawled lassie of yesteryear be shocked by mini-skirts, trouser-suits or teenage jeans, or just envious? The reaction of the pre-1914 short-haired, clean-shaven, hard collared male to the leather jackets, high heeled boots, and shoulder-length hair of late-20th century man is more predictable. Certainly society today is less class-conscious, although it has been claimed that, despite the existence in the mid-19th century of several different classes, or strata, of society, nevertheless each class took a kindly, but perhaps patronising interest in the others. There were the Highland 'Gentry' and their families; then the professional class, the clergy, solicitors, doctors, bankers; next the 'bourgeoisie' shopowners, often quite prosperous; the artisans and skilled tradesmen; and finally the casual labourers, whose families lived just above subsistence level. Folk in those days were, it seems, less impersonal and more demonstrative in their human relationships than now; friendships were closer, more intimate, and adults were less inhibited in displaying emotion in public. At Victorian funerals, for example, mourning and sorrow was deeply felt and men and women wept openly. However, in those times there was a callous attitude to animals, both domestic and wild, and an enthusiasm for blood-sports and game-shooting, with large 'bags' of creatures great and small, indiscriminately destroyed, which would horrify most people today.

Perhaps because our 19th century forebears led less complex lives, they all the more laughed and expressed pleasure and enjoyed practical jokes. But this is not to say that the Victorians and Edwardians were simple souls, or devoid of intellect. You have only to read the fine volumes of the Transactions of Inverness Field Club to realise the quality of mind, the industrious research and the progressive reasoning of our predecessors. The sheer erudition of these intelligent men typifies the Victorian. Even in the midst of our country's sophisticated technology we have to admit that little advance has been made on the epoch-making inventions of the 19th century — amongst others, photography, electricity, telephone, internal combustion engine, gramophone, wireless, cinema, aeronautics, modern medicine and drugs — the list is long.

So how did our Victorians and Edwardians live and spend their days? Undoubtedly they were less healthy than we are: consumption, diphtheria and other killer diseases took their toll and people lived shorter lives, though not necessarily less happy ones. Smoking tobacco in the 1850s was minimal compared to the menace to health it has become today. In the 1880s few married men and almost no women smoked. About 90% of tobacco was then consumed in pipes — mostly clays — and the rest as cigars and snuff. Cigarettes were seldom smoked before 1900, for their great rise in popularity dates from the First World War. The 19th century working day was longer, Saturday was not a day off, and annual holidays were shorter, although there were numerous Fast Days. Employers were harsher to their staff, trade unions were in their infancy. Industry and business was controlled by private enterprise, there were few monopolies and multi-national combines, and little bureaucratic control by the State. Income Tax was negligible, and VAT was not even dreamed about.

The Christian religion meant more to people then. The clergy were an extremely privileged class, looked up to as doctors were till recently. The Sabbath was sacrosanct to all the many sects of Presbyterianism, and no work, no play, no normal activity on the day of rest was possible under the eye of the omnipotent Kirk, its minister and its session — even the Sunday meals had to be cooked on Saturday, and eaten cold the next day. It was not until after the First World War that the Kirk's power began to wane, and by then most churches had introduced Sunday Schools, woman's guilds, and other social institutions.

But despite hard toil and working conditions, diseases and the inhibitions of religious fervour, the folk of Inverness and the Highlands could be said to have led reasonably happy lives. Many commodities of life, and lots of luxuries were comparatively cheap by today's standards. The town had a relaxed, almost lazy air about its thoroughfares; no rush of traffic save the odd horse-carriage bowling along, bearing a Highland laird, or a top-hatted lawyer on his way to the Court House, or a doctor to see his patients. A tinkling bicycle-bell was often the only sound to strike the ear of a bystander or a stroller on the dusty streets. There were cab stances at the Exchange and at the Station, but these were patronised more by travellers and visitors: the town's few streets meant that it was but a short walk from the Ness Bridge to Petty Street, or from the Maggot to the Castle Hill — and in those days 'Shank's mare' was the only transport most folk had. A fleet of street sweepers, or 'scaffies', with hurleys and brooms was required to cleanse the streets of horse-dung. Horses were watered at troughs sited in High Street and elsewhere. Message-boys whistled as they trundled handcarts. Burly constables of Highland descent strutted along, only to be outshone by the more dashing and colourful uniforms of soldiers of the Militia or the Volunteers. When the gloaming came the 'leerie' made his rounds, lighting up the gas-lamps along the streets.

As most of the citizens were from the Highlands, there were many social events, with hospitality, dancing, and a 'ceilidh', or 'at home', where, before the days of cinema, radio and television, families and guests made their own entertainment, singing the old traditional songs round a piano. Or a fiddler or two would play at dances, often held in private houses — thus many a courtship started, when today it more likely happens at a disco. But the highlight of the social year was the Northern Meeting Ball — instituted in 1788 — which followed the Northern Meeting Games, then a very much more Highland event than today, and patronised by clan chiefs and lairds and their families in full Highland dress, joined by Invernessians similarly turned out for the great occasion to enjoy the piping, dancing and athletic competitions.

The second half of the 19th century saw the growth of organised spectator sports in Inverness, as elsewhere. All the local association football teams each had their own partisan following of fans. Camanachd, or shinty, that ancient and robust Highland game, never lost its popularity and it is played in Inverness as elsewhere throughout the Gaidhealtachd. Rugby football, cricket and hockey clubs were founded in more recent times. However despite the increase in games-watching, there have always been those who believe in keeping fit by various forms of personal exercise. Bicycling was extremely popular in the first decade of this century, skating was a winter-sport, like curling, at Loch na Sanais, Torvean. Inverness Tennis Club, on Bishop's Road, was founded in 1892: there were public and private bowling greens from the turn of the century, that in Bishop's Road was founded in 1874. Inverness Golf Club, dating from 1883, has its course at Culcabock — golf was also played at the Longman until the Second World War. Swimming was catered for by public baths at Montague Row until the General Strike, followed by coal shortage, closed the pool in 1927. The present Swimming Baths opened in 1936, and Inverness produced several swimming stars, including an Olympic water-polo gold medallist between the wars.

At Dunain Park outside the town the Inverness Horse Races were held during Edwardian times and up to the First World War. To Invernessians angling on the Ness was always a popular sport, and it is a unique feature of the town that you can see a salmon played and landed as traffic roars busily along the riverside. Since the Middle Ages Inverness has owned a priceless and beautiful recreation area at the Ness Islands — so far virtually unspoilt and unexploited. Here from early ages the burgh magnates entertained their guests — and themselves — with lavish banquets. In Victorian times the circus's coming to the town was a great event, particularly for the youngsters and theatrical drama, though not really approved by the Kirk, became more and more popular, the main theatre being the Theatre Royal, Bank Street, which was destroyed by fire in the early 1930s. By the First World War the cinema drew audiences away from the theatre. During the thirties the town had four cinemas — the Playhouse (burnt down and demolished 1972), the Palace (now a bingo-hall), the La Scala (still with us), and the Empire Theatre (used also as a cinema) which survived demolition till 1971, and catered, despite its imperfect acoustics, for audiences for orchestral concerts, opera, ballet, and other minority-appeal entertainments.

By the first decade of the 20th century youth organisations — Boy's Brigade, Boy Scouts, and Girl Guides — had their followings in Inverness. The 1914-18 War brought tragic losses to nearly every family in the town: many of the killed and wounded serving with the Seaforth Highlanders, the Cameron Highlanders, and the Lovat Scouts. The Second World War of 1939-45 made itself felt much nearer home. Inverness was virtually a garrison town. Dalcross and the Longman aerodromes were bases for the war in the air. A large part of the Highlands north and west of the Caledonian Canal was a Protected Area, entry to which could be obtained only by possession of a permit. A postal and telephone censorship department was established in Inverness.

After the forties, due to the general economic stability and the benefits of the

'Welfare State', most people found themselves part of the 'affluent society', one of the advantages of which was more time for leisure activities. These took many forms: some pursued the sport or pastime of their choice, others patronised the clubs, associations and learned societies founded in Victorian and Edwardian times. Of these, the Inverness Scientific Society and Field Club, instituted in 1875, has nowadays, as the Inverness Field Club, more members and support than it ever had. It original interests were in Geology, Botany, Natural History and Archaeology — and these remain its chief pursuits — but its real importance is that it was ahead of its time as a forerunner which led directly to the formation of modern pressure groups involved with taking positive action concerning conservation and the protection of the environment. These groups are also the result of the need for more and more public vigilance and participation to reverse the effects of bureaucratic control, and thus to improve the amenities of our surroundings and safeguard the quality of the way of life in Inverness and the Highlands in the present and for the future.

EDWARD MELDRUM
*President,*
Inverness Field Club.


# AS OTHERS SEE US

*This castle hath a pleasant seat; the air*
*Nimbly and sweetly recommends itself*
*Unto our gentle sense. This guest of summer*
*The temple-haunting martlet, does approve*
*By his loved masonry, that the heaven's breath*
*Smells wooingly here; no jutty, frieze,*
*Buttress, nor coigne of vantage, but this bird*
*Hath made his pendent bed and procreant cradle.*
*Where they most breed and haunt, I have observed,*
*The air is delicate.*

SHAKESPEARE, c. 1605.

*"After church, we walked down the Quay. We then went to Macbeth's castle. I had a romantic satisfaction in seeing Dr Johnson actually in it. It perfectly corresponds with Shakespeare's description."*

BOSWELL, 1773.

*"While I was in Inverness there was not a trace of its ancient castle; some person having lately removed the small remains of its ruins to build offices, or some such thing, for his own convenience: What a Hottentot!"*

SARAH MURRAY, 1799.

1

2

Success, the train, with two engines to make sure of arriving, creeps steadily through the drifts with a triumphant plume of smoke from the leading smoke-stack. The flattened smoke shows that the gales were still blowing. No nonsense about diesel or electric powered engines then.

**3**

The old Town House, built in 1708 as the town house of Lord Lovat, became the Burgh Town House in 1716. Beyond is the Commercial Hotel, formerly The Horns, where Boswell and Johnson stayed in September, 1773.

All that was left of the old Town House after demolition in 1878.

**5**

The present Town House. In the Council Chamber the Cabinet met on 7 September, 1921, under David Lloyd George, to discuss the Irish Question, the only time that the Cabinet has met outside London.

**4**

*Of the buildings seen in this picture, only the Steeple and the adjacent Court House still stand. Gordon's Place, the cottages in the right foreground, which replaced Castle Tolmie (demolished after 1849), were themselves pulled down for the second "Castle Tolmie."*

6

*The corner building has gone, but the second "Castle Tolmie", built by Robert Carruthers, is still standing in this picture. Among its other occupants was Mr Gossip, the dentist. It was demolished in the 1960s.*

7

*The temporary bridge for traffic, used while the new bridge was being built. The older part of the Castle (1834) is on the right, the later (1846) on the left.*

8

*A Horse Fair on Bank Street, July 1928.*

*Queen Mary's House, the white house built on the site of the house in which Queen Mary is supposed to have stayed in 1562. It was demolished in the 1960s and the present Highlands and Islands Development Board building put on the site. The demolition on the south side of Bridge Street is clearly seen.*

9

10

**11**

*Photograph by George Washington Wilson, taken from a building now demolished.*

**12**

*The corner of the High Street and Inglis Street. The steps on the left are known as Market Brae or Post Office Steps.*

**13**

*The High Street in the 1920s. The figures on the YMCA building at the corner of Castle Street are Faith, Hope and Charity. They are now at Graemeshall in Orkney.*

**14**

*The Royal Tartan Warehouse has its shutters closed, but is decorated for some Royal Event. The carved arms in the gable are the Scottish Royal Arms.*

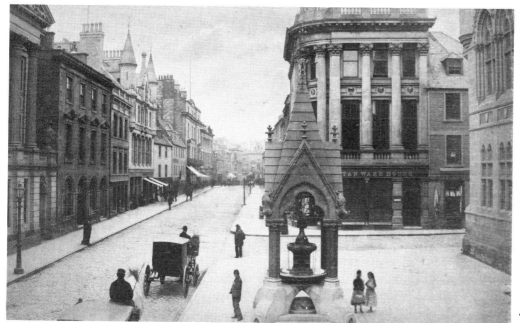

In the foreground is the Exchange, the centre of Inverness. Under the memorial fountain (now in the Cavell Gardens east of the river) is the Clach-na-cuddain (the Stone of the Tubs), the palladium of Inverness. It is now mounted against the wall of the Town House, as it used to be, see 3 and 5.

15

16

The Station Square in the early years of the 20th century. The Station Hotel has a handsome dome, now vanished, and the buildings containing the Board Room of the old Highland Railway Company have been built on the north side. Compare number 19.

*The corner of Church Street and Academy Street, just before the 1939 War. The spire of the Free North Church can be seen behind the Technical School.*

*Academy Street, showing the Empire Theatre or The Picture House. The tower of the East Church, on the left, was designed by Alexander Ross.*

17

18

**19**

*Station Square about 1883. A Boys' Choir is singing and presumably the photograph was taken by A. W. Fraser, since his "studio" is so clearly brought out.*

*A busy scene in Queensgate. The previous Post Office building, demolished in 1966, is on the right.*

**20**

**21**

*Dalcross's House, built in 1700 on the corner of Church Street and Queensgate is about to be demolished to make way for the present Clydesdale Bank. The carved stones above the dormer windows are preserved in the Bank.*

**22**

The Steeple, built in 1791, by William Sibbald. The upper part was bent in the earthquake of 1816 and had to be rebuilt. It is said that the larger of the balls beneath the weathercock contains two gallons of whisky.

*Lifting the setts in Church Street. This was before the demolition of Bridge Street was complete.*

**23**

The gateway from Church Street to the Old High Church. The house on the left has now been put into good order by the National Trust for Scotland. The corner of the Grey Friars Church can be seen on the right.

24

25

The Technical school on the right was demolished during the 1970s. It adjoins the Grey Friars' Church. The top of the Old High Church can be seen on the right.

*This close, or vennel, runs from the east side of Church Street, opposite the Old High Church gate, to Academy Street, where a gable of the A.I. Welders' building can be seen, with its mosaic of work in the arch.*

26

27

*The courtyard at Bow Court before restoration began, looking towards Church Street. Many of the vanished older houses were built round such courts, on to which their various doors opened.*

*"House in Church Street in course of removal on site occupied by A. McDonald's Property,"* wrote Alexander Ross, identifying Jas. Rose and F. McRae to the left of the ladder, Andw. McD and A. Ross to the right.

**28**

*Abertarff's House before the houses on the right were removed and it was opened to Church Street. The oldest surviving house in Inverness, it was built in 1593 and was the town house of the Frasers of Abertarff, among others. Restored by the National Trust for Scotland, it is now occupied by An Comunn Gaidhealach.*

Dunbar's Hospital, "an ancient-looking house, said to have been built of the materials of Cromwell's Fort . . . was bequeathed to the community by Provost Dunbar in 1668, but was afterwards used as a grammar-school till the opening of the Royal Academy in 1792 . . . the building was then divided to serve as a parish library, female school, female work society . . . the ground floor being occupied by the fire engines. During the time that the cholera raged in Inverness, part of it again served as a hospital."

30

31

Bow Court. Only School Lane divides this from Dunbar's Hospital. It was probably built about 1729 by Katherine Duff, Lady Drummuir, as a tablet on the wall in School Lane shows. Both these buildings have had work done on them since these photographs were taken. Bow Court was reconstructed in 1972 as shops and flats, one retaining some of the original panelling. William Glashan was the restoring architect.

**32**

*The Old High Church. Only the tower remains of the mediaeval parish church of Inverness, and this is surmounted by an 18th century parapet and tower. The church was rebuilt in 1770 and known as the English Church, no Gaelic being used in the services. The cottages to the left of the grassy bank were demolished in the 1970s.*

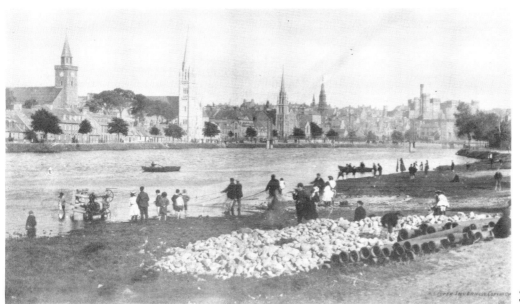

**33**

**34**

*A closer view of Bank Street. Only the Castle, the Steeple, St Columba High Church and, of course, the Courier Office, the building to the right of the carriages, now survive.*

*Friars' Street. Behind the wall on the left may still be found a burying ground and the one surviving pillar of the Dominican Friary. These Black Friars (so named from their robes) also gave their name to the Friars' Shott. All the houses on the left have been demolished and replaced by vast Telephone Exchanges. In the burying ground are several interesting monuments, the earliest may be that of Alexander Stewart, Earl of Mar and Justiciar of the North, who died in 1435.*

**36**

*Raining's School, built in 1757 and named after Dr Raining of Norwich, who left money to that end. In 1963, when this picture was taken, it was used by the Youth Club, but it has now been demolished to enlarge a car park.*

**37**

*Raining's Stairs lead from Ardconnel Street to Castle Street and show the steepness of the Escarpment. The houses on the right have now largely gone.*

Many of these old roofs can still be seen above the shop fronts. This picture shows how steeply the Escarpment rises behind the houses in Castle Street.

Looking north along Castle Street before the houses on the left were pulled down. The Castle Street Gate may have been about here.

40

41

42

Above left: Collapse of the bank to the east of the Castle in 1932. The archway through to the Police Station has since been demolished.

Above: "In front of the Police Office (in the Castle Wynd) we pause for a moment while we stand over the grave of the last criminal hung in Inverness — John Adams, who was executed in 1835" John Fraser, 1905.

Left: "How great was the fall thereof." One third of the Burgh's Road Department is a casualty of the landslide at the Castle, see No. 117.

*St Andrew's Cathedral, designed and drawn by Alexander Ross, architect. The spires were never built.*

"The Foundation stone of the 'new St John's' was laid on the 31 March, 1837, by the Reverend Charles Fyvie . . . and the church was finished and opened in July 1838. The roof is modelled on that of Henry VII's Chapel in Westminster Abbey. In the eyes of the congregation who at that time worshipped within its walls, the beautiful, comfortable and quiet little church, with its simplicity and soft, subdued light, was considered perfect." It cost £2000 to build and was demolished in 1903, but the tower remained in Church Street until 1958.

**44**

**45**

The Choir of St Andrew's Cathedral as it was originally built to the design of Alexander Ross. It was altered after 1918, to accommodate the memorial Rood and Screen.

View from Tomnahurich, showing Park House in the right foreground, the Royal Northern Infirmary in the centre and, across the river, the path leading up the Escarpment to Godsman's Walk. The Crown School is on the left, almost on the skyline.

From Tomnahurich to the sea. This picture dates from before the development of Victoria Park, in the foreground, for there is no bandstand. The Northern Meeting Ground is seen over the trees on the Glen Urquhart road.

*The Cathedral and Palace, both designed by Dr Alexander Ross. The foundation stone of the Cathedral was laid in 1866 and it was dedicated in 1869 and consecrated (being by then free of debt) in 1874. Eden Court, where the Bishop used to live, was named for Robert Eden (Bishop 1851-86) and is now part of the Eden Court Theatre complex.*

49

*Ardross Terrace, also by Alexander Ross, showing how the empty land near the Cathedral has been built over the last hundred years. Only the Cathedral and Craig Dunain Hospital, on the hill to the right, appear in both.*

*Duff Street, above, and Chisholm's Close, on the west side of the river, as they were in 1900. The thatched roofs are already being replaced by slates, and there is gas lighting in the streets.*

*A group of carpenters and their families. The children seem to have been playing cricket barefoot in the road. Notice the water-pump at the edge of the pavement.*

**52**

**53**

*Bissets Close — showing how snug cottages deteriorate when left without occupants.*

*Hamilton's Auction Mart in 1896 (above) and in 1972 (below) after the new sales ring and offices had been built.*

Drakies Toll House used to stand near where the entrance to Raigmore Hospital now is.

Behind Inshes House is this Barmkin Tower, all that remains of the 16th century castle of the Robertsons of Inshes.

*The Glen Albyn Distillery reflected in the water of the Muirtown Basin.*

58

*Kingsmills, before the cottages in the background were demolished.*

59

**60**

*After the fire, workmen on the facade of the Waverley Hotel, where the early meetings of the Inverness Field Club were held. Now it is the Douglas Hotel, in Union Street.*

**61**

*Workmen inspecting the new sewer at Clachnaharry.*

**62**

**63**

*Two scenes of winter which cover between them, but only just, the three suspension bridges. The temporary bridge can be seen behind the Ness Bridge.*

**64**

*The attack on Bridge Street begins. Behind the cables of the bridge, on the right, is Castle Tolmie. On the left is Queen Mary's House. The later part (1846) of the Castle is above.*

*Bridge Street in the early years of the century. Every building seen in the street has now been demolished.*

*The End of Bridge Street (1965). Looming through the stour stands the Steeple, but its neighbour, the Workman's Club, has almost gone.*

The old Caledonian Hotel was built in 1780 with money from the Forfeited Estates to improve the meeting place of the St John's Masonic Lodge and enlarged by them in 1822 at a further cost of £2000, and again in 1882 for £6000. It was demolished in the 1960s and replaced by the present building.

67

68

Destruction and Construction of the Ness Bridge. The old archway has almost gone, and the coffer dam for the east pier is being built. Queen Mary's House is on the left. The new bridge won a Saltire Award.

*The End of the Workman's Club (1965). Behind, Faith, Hope and Charity have vanished from the corner of Church Street.*

## 70

*When Britain ruled the waves. The Channel Fleet in the Inverness Firth in 1854 or 1855.*

*The Harbour in about 1896, with a collier in the middle.*

## 71

*The Swedish "Sverre" lying in Muirtown Basin about 1893.*

## 72

**73**

*Inverness Harbour at about the end of the last century. The Harbour-Master's Office is the small building to the right of the scyamore tree.*

**74**

*The old repairing dock, which was part of the moat of Cromwell's Fort. It was filled in entirely about 1900. The small steamer is the Warlock and the Harbour-Master, Captain William Morrison, is in the rowing boat.*

**75**

*The sycamore tree was cut down fifty years or more ago. It sheltered Citadel House. The building to the left of the tree was the Fever Hospital. The tower on the left is now surrounded by fuel tanks.*

Muirtown Locks. Locking a fishing boat up from Muirtown Basin, on passage to the west coast.

77

Washing skins on the river. This was a part of the Tanning at Chisholm's Tannery, near-by. It was unpopular with fishermen, as it was thought to pollute the water.

*Loch Ness, a paddle steamer, and Ethel tied up at Muirtown at the top of the locks.*

*Gondolier, all tilted over by the passengers making for the gangway, comes in to the landing stage at the end of a journey from Fort Augustus.*

*The Thornbush Slipway being built in 1908 for the Rose Street Foundry, who built and repaired drifters and trawlers there. The old windmill can be seen without its sails in the background to the right.*

**80**

**81**

*A drifter on the Slipway at the Thornbush.*

**82**

*The Marine Engineering Shop of the Rose Street Foundry, now A.I. Welders. It was here that all the welding machines for Operation PLUTO were made. They joined 70 miles of 3 inch piping to supply the Allied Forces after D-Day in 1944.*

**83**

*Workmen with a drifter built at Thornbush Quay, west of the river, and ready for her launch.*

84

*The Inverness Printers' section of the parade through the town to celebrate the passing of the Third Reform Bill in 1885.*

*The Printers in the Printing Works of the Inverness Courier before 1914.*

85

**86**

*The Staff of the Royal Northern Infirmary on 17 May, 1929, when the Duke and Duchess of York (The Earl and Countess of Inverness) later their Majesties King George VI and Queen Elizabeth, opened the new buildings.*

**87**

*Mr Kincaid, the Clachnaharry Blacksmith, in his smithy in 1968.*

**88**

*Clachnaharry, with the older part of the village to the left of the railway line. The canal reaches the sea just above the chimneys and beyond the shallow water is South Kessock with the ferry to the Black Isle.*

89   *The Burgh Police, 3rd July, 1910. "Highlanders every one and of a class of which the Highlands may feel proud, stalwart men all, of powerful build, and of a high average of intelligence, the safety and peace of our town is safe in their hands." Chief Constable John McNaughton is seated in the middle of the front row.*

90

*Police Inspection, 20 September, 1937. Left to right, Bailie Joseph MacLeod; Provost Hugh Mackenzie; Mr James Cameron, Town Clerk (rear); Brigadier General Dudgeon, Chief Inspector of Police; Councillor D.G. Campbell (rear); Chief Constable Neville.*

*Mrs Playne-Smith, of Drummond Park, whose peacocks and donkeys are still remembered, used to give a dram and some shortbread to every cabby at Christmas. This shows the ceremony.*

*James Duncan, Fern Villa, Inverness, was a traveller in soft goods. He kept his ponies at Drakies, and this pair were bred by G. R. Linklater, of Weisdale, Shetland. The dwarf was known as Neil. The scene is at Heathmount in 1890.*

**92**

**93**

*Milk Float outside the west door of the Cathedral. The milk came in the large churns and was measured out into the family jugs as needed. There were no bottles.*

**94**

*The heavy cart horse, the main motive power on the farms, walks down Bridge Street in 1962 after a visit to the blacksmith.*

**95**

*Highland Railway Engine. It appears to be Number 1 and its name, "Raigmore", commemorates one of the original committee, Mr Mackintosh of Raigmore.*

**96**

*02/467 4-4-0 No. 79 "Atholl" standing by the loco box at Inverness. It is decorated for moving a Royal Train, presumably to carry Queen Victoria. The driver and fireman wear bowler hats, and those on "Raigmore" wear toppers.*

Coal being taken to the town from the harbour by a horse-drawn cart running on the rails.

98

The Duke of Sutherland's private sleeping-coach, drawn by "Dunrobin."

*Left: The "Sverre" passing through the Kessock Narrows on her way to the Harbour in 1895.*

*Below left: A Ferry Pilot. This is another of Alexander Dallas pictures on glass plates.*

*Below: The Kessock Ferry nearing South Kessock with a good load, around 1900.*

*Kessock Ferry. The sailing ferry has been replaced.*

103

*Ewen Dallas with his Penny Farthing bicycle. He was one of a talented family, which included Alexander Dallas, a first rate photographer, and Danny, the well-known entertainer.*

104

*Cyclists at the Muirtown Hotel. On the left is a man's bicycle with a bar, on the right is a lady's safety bicycle, with cords from the rear mudguard to the hub so that the long skirts did not get entangled in the wheel.*

*Left: May Queen, one of Macrae and Dick's coaches, about to set out for Culloden. The driver is Mr John Mackay and the Bugler, Mr Peter Tronnery, is standing with his Post Horn, near the rear wheel.*

*Below: At the end of the 19th century bicycling was all the rage. Some say that it was the beginning of Woman's Liberation, the young people all rode off in groups, as here.*

105

106

**107**

*The first car in Inverness, before the days of number plates. It later became ST6. It belonged to Dr England Kerr and is here in the hands of his sisters, "Aunt Aggie, Aunt Hester and Aunt Lottie." When it was first seen, it was a marvel, "on it rolled, all on its own, no horse, no-one pushing."*

**108**

*The doctors' cars at South Kessock. ST7 Driver Cameron, Doctor Nicholson. ST6, Doctor Brown. ST8, Driver Whyte, Doctor G.W. England Kerr.*

The Whitebridge Post Bus, an Albion, at the Post Office in Queensgate. It carried passengers as well as the mail, now "just invented" and "the latest thing" of the 1870s. The conductor, with x on his cap, is Mr Murdo Fraser, late of Fraser and Eland's garage, now S.M.T.

109

110

The Glenurquhart Bus, which was owned by the people of the Glen, about 1910. The driver is Mr J. Horsburgh, standing by him are Mr J. Gordon (draper, Inverness) and Mr MacDougall (Drumnadrochit). The others include Mr D. Macmillan (Oakbank) conductor, Mr D. Mackenzie (Achtemerack) and Mr A. Ross (Tomatin).

*Mr Roderick Macrae (below) and Mr William Dick joined forces in 1878 to provide "First class open or closed carriages, Landaus, Wagonettes, Transport Carts, Phaetons, Dog Carts and Gigs." Today their names are known all over the North as Motor Engineers.*

**112**

**111**

*Early days in Macrae and Dick's motor workshops.*

*The District Nurse takes to powered transport — a distinct improvement on her push-bike or feet. This was the first round Inverness.*

115

**116**

*The first £100 Car, which Lady Burton bought. It was a Ford 8. Standing beside the car are Mr Cameron, from Harris, the Manager of A. W. Chapman, Mr Fowke, representing Highland Transport, and, to the left of the bicycle, Mr Grant, Sales Manager.*

*This 1921 Vulcan, ST1410, was the Ferry Bus owned by W. Greig. M. Greig is the Conductor. It was the first bus in Inverness to have pneumatic tyres, its speed was 12 m.p.h.*

117

118

*A 30/60 H.P. 29-seater Passenger Rear-entrance Bus, which came to Inverness on 18 May, 1926.*

*Mr James Fraser, standing on the lorry, with the two Burgh Roads Department lorries. The "fleet" was completed by the steam roller, see 42. The cottages are now demolished.*

*Chapman's Garage in Eastgate. The manager, sitting, in front, is Mr Fowke.*

*The first flight of the Inverness Gliding Club's first glider, on 27 May, 1936, on the Longman Airfield.*

*The Longman Airfield in 1948. "If Invernessians of the future exhibit the same energy and industry as those of today (1905), it will not be surprising if this locality turns out one of the most flourishing centres of industry in the North . . . If the landscape all round is not studded with thriving factories 50 or 60 years hence, it will be be because the wheel of progress has stopped short."*

*Aerial view from over the Longman. The outline of Cromwell's Fort can still be made out in the right foreground, but the first of the fuel tanks have appeared and in front of Tomnahurich, houses are growing.*

**123**

**124**

*Kingsmills district from the air. The golf course is in the lower right corner and the football ground of Inverness Thistle in the centre.*

*De Havilland 89 Air Liner which flew between Inverness and Shetland in 1936.*

**125**

**126**

*G-ADCT Dragon preparing to come in to land on the Longman Airfield in 1934 with a patient from the Western Isles. This was the first Air Ambulance in the Highlands.*

*The ebb-tide running out under Mitchell's railway bridge into the harbour.*

**127**

**128**

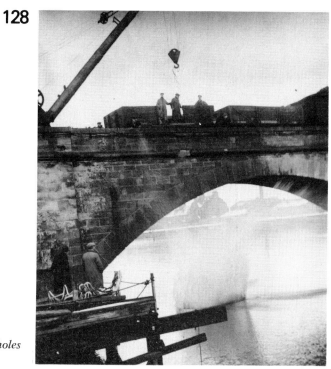

*Depositing ballast upstream of the railway bridge to fill the holes scoured out by the force of the river.*

*Floods in July, 1956, left, on the A9 at the top of Culcabock Brae. Raigmore Hospital is behind the houses on the left. Below, at the bottom of the brae, where the Millburn roundabout now is. "I have often thought that the climate of Inverness might be used to more purpose in advertising the town as a holiday resort. Our rainfall is among the lowest in Scotland; our temperature, especially in winter, is high, while our freedom from thunderstorms is remarkable."*

129

130

*Raigmore House in 1963, built by Archibald Simpson, architect, Aberdeen, for Mackintosh of Raigmore. Demolished 1965.*

131

132

*Crown House in 1962, formerly known as Abertarff's House, being the town house of the Frasers of Abertarff. Permission to demolish this western wing, which is balanced on the east by a matching wing, was given by the District Council in 1977, and perpetrated in 1978.*

*Heatherley was a well-known school for girls from 1915 until 1956, when Miss Bedale retired. The house has now been divided into flats.*

133

134

*Balnain House dates from the first half of the 18th century. "The 'Blue House' in Huntly Street — so named from its being one of the first slated houses in the town . . . is now turned into a lodging house for the poor, who bleach their clothes on the space in front which was once secluded from the public gaze by fine old trees and shrubs." It is now to be restored.*

**135**

*Masonic Room. St John Kilwinning Lodge "is an ancient institution, but its minutes and property were lost in the Rebellion of 1745. To improve their place of meeting, a grant of money was obtained in 1780 from the Commissioners of Forfeited Estates to assist in erecting a new hotel and lodge; hence the existence of the Caledonian Hotel."*

*James Barron, junior, the son of James Barron of the Courier, and father of Miss Eveline Barron, now of the Courier.*

*The Parlour of the home of the Dallas family, 4 Hill Place, before the gas lighting was installed.*

*Grey Friars Church. Rebuilt in 1792, this is now a Free Church. It was called The Gaelic Church, because nothing but English was used in the High Church. The old pulpit, on the left, known as The Black Pulpit, was removed to a warehouse for safe-keeping after the Free Church took over the building, but vandals got in and smashed it to pieces. There never were Franciscan Friars in Inverness, so why their nick-name, "Grey Friars," has been accepted is a mystery.*

**139**

*The Museum, which, with the Public Library, was largely the result of the enthusiasm and gifts and loans of the members of the Field Club, who met there most years in their first fifty years to look over the latest acquisitions and decide what gaps should be filled. In 1977 the reorganised Museum was second only to the Royal Scottish Museum as the best museum in Scotland.*

*Laying the Foundation Stone of the Academy on the Crown in 1895, with a full turn-out of Masons. Dr Alexander Ross can be seen at "about two o'clock" from the stone, holding his top hat.*

140

141

*The completed Academy on the Crown. More has been added behind these buildings, and a new extension was opened at Culduthel in April 1978.*

142

*Assembly for prayers in the Hall of the Academy. Only the Upper School is here, and less than half are in the picture. The Staff sit against the walls.*

*The Hall later in the day. The Staff are having their "Elevenses."* 143

The Staff of the Academy in about 1892. Back row, left to right, Miss Mary C. Mackenzie, Assist. Art; Mr William Gossip, Junior English; Miss Cosy Fraser, Pianoforte; Mons. Pierre Delavault, Art Master; Mr Charles G. H. Greaves, English and Commercial Master; Mr W. S. Roddie, Singing Master; Mr Wallace, Assist. Elementary Dept. Front row, Miss Grace Middleton, Sewing Mistress; Mons. Edouard Roubaut, Modern Languages Master; Miss Brown, Lady Superintendant; Mr George T. Bruce, Rector (English); Mr Thomas Cockburn, Classical Master; Miss Clegg, Assist. Elementary Dept.; Mr Reid, Maths Master.

Large Art Room, Royal Academy.

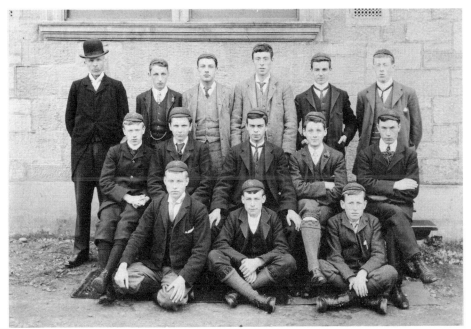

Class VI Classics, 1902 or 1903. Back row, Mr T. Cockburn, Classics Master; The Revd. Dr R. T. Cameron, Aberdeen; The Revd. Percy Mackenzie, London; "Big MacInnes," Roderick MacInnes, Raasay; The Revd. Alister Stewart, Paisley Abbey; Ian Mackay, U.F. Manse, Fort Augustus, Captain of Academy 1903. Middle row, H. Gallie Scott, M.A., LL.D., Captain of Academy 1902, Vancouver, Canada; Professor J. Maclean, Madras, "Flashy"; Dr J.J. Mackintosh; Professor John Baillie; G. Macfaddyen, Civil Engineer. Front row, The Revd. Angus Nicolson, Lawers; —. Macdonald?, Scaniport; Dan Maclachlan, Beauly.

Class VI Girls, 1902 or 1903. No names are given.

**148**

*The last parade of the Volunteers of 1859, in Farraline Park (in 1885). Behind the parade is Dr Bell's Institution, built in Greek Revival Style. There were once gardens in front of the school. Now they are the Bus Station and a Car Park.*

*The Northern Counties Collegiate School, designed in 1873 by Alexander Ross. It ended in 1914 and was bought as a War Memorial Hostel by the Royal Academy in 1921. It is now part of the Highland Regional Buildings.*

**149**

**150**

*The Inverness Militia, who later became the 3rd Battalion, Cameron Highlanders.*

# SHOOTING GALLERY,
## CHURCH STREET.

### MR. J. WINK

BEGS to return his best thanks to his numerous Friends for the very liberal patronage bestowed on him since his arrival in Inverness, and, at the request of a number of Friends, he is to remain a short time longer, and has now to intimate that Practice Shooting commences again THIS DAY (Monday, 28th inst.)

MR. J. WINK, as a further inducement, intimates that he will put up TWO LEGS of MUTTON each day to be shot for — Twopence per Shot.

Those not disposed to compete for the Mutton, can have Rifle Practice as usual—1d. each.

INVERNESS, 86, CHURCH STREET.
28th April, 1845.

W. & A. JOHNSTON, Printers, 78, Church Street, Inverness.

**151**

*Mr Wink's Shooting Gallery was clearly a popular visitor to Inverness in April, 1845.*

**152**

*The Fire Brigade about 1890.*

**153** *Volunteers in their annual camp before 1914. In the centre is Alexander Dallas.*

**154**

*September, 1939, more Volunteers. Members of the Auxiliary Territorial Service called up to duty at Cameron Barracks a day or two before the war began. Left to right, standing, Miss M. Mitchell, Miss A. Watson, Miss M. Fraser; sitting, Miss C. Chisholm, Miss F. MacGregor and Miss C. Duncan. Bananas were going to be unobtainable.*

**155**

*American Supply Ship 1917/18. During the War no one was allowed to take a camera north of the Ferry, nor to take a photograph. "My father, Alexander Dallas, did so and took this photograph," says Miss Dallas. "I think it must be a rather rare picture. When the ships went out to sea, the crews were silent, on their return they were shouting and singing. We put it down to cowardice."*

*Field Marshal Lord Montgomery of Alamein inspecting the Guard of Honour of the Queen's Own Cameron Highlanders at the Depot in November, 1946.*

156

157

*The last march through the town of the Queen's Own Cameron Highlanders, Freemen of the Burgh, with colours flying and band playing, before the amalgamation of the Seaforth Highlanders with the Camerons to form the Queen's Own Highlanders in 1961.*

The completed statue to the fallen of the Queen's Own Cameron Highlanders in the wars in Egypt and the Sudan. It stands today in the Station Square, where it was unveiled in 1892. The Sculptor was G. Wade, of London.

*Great grandmother Ann Mackintosh or Macdonald, born 1821, died 1890.*
*See her descendants on next page, No. 160.*

*Great Grandfather Macdonald with his children and grandchildren in 1895.*

*The Donald family in their 1916 Cadillac.*

*Left to right at A.I. Welders, Mr Sam Hunter Gordon with three generations of workers, Mr David Forbes, his son Mr Dai Forbes and his grandson Mr Terry McDonnagh.*

163

*Two Field Club outings. Dr Alexander Ross is in both. Dr William Mackay may be the member in the middle of the top picture, pointing out something*

164

**165**

**166**

*Dr Thomas Aitken, M.D., was the first Superintendant of Craig Dunain, and was there from 1864 to 1892. He had "identified himself with the whole history of the Institution and done his work most faithfully and zealously." He wrote the letter to the Courier which resulted in the foundation of the Inverness Scientific Society and Field Club in 1875 and compiled a list of plants for the first volume of the Transactions.*

*Sir Murdoch Macdonald, K.C.M.G., C.B. Member of Parliament for Inverness-shire. He was made a Freeman of Inverness on the same day as Ramsay Macdonald, then Prime Minister, and Stanley Baldwin a past and future Prime Minister, whose mother was a Macdonald.*

167

*Two Field Club Outings to Essich, the top one, before 1914, includes Sir Henry Munro, Dr Alexander Ross, Mr James Barron, ex-Provost Gossip and Mr Duncan Campbell, all of whom were dead by the second visit to Essich on 8 August, 1925.*

168

*James Barron, of the Inverness Courier and General Advertiser for the Counties of Inverness, Ross, Moray, Nairn, Cromarty, Sutherland and Caithness, to give its original and continuing name, though Cromarty has moved up in the list. Born in the parish of Edinkille in Moray in 1847, he joined the Courier in 1865 and after 1873 was the working editor. By 1910 he had become the sole proprietor. He died in February, 1919. He was a Founder-member of the Field Club of which he was twice President and was editor of the Transactions from 1875 almost up to his death.*

*"Forty Pockets."*

**171**

*Dr Alexander Ross, architect. Provost of Inverness 1889-95, he was born in the reign of William IV and died in 1925. He has been called "the Sir Christopher Wren of the North" and his buildings may be seen all over the Highlands.*

**172**

*The Ross family at Riverdale, now Ach-an-Eas, Island Bank Road.*

Alexander Ross  Mary Ann Ross

Dollie                 Mary

Aunt Ann      Mabel                Jane

Mrs Ross  Alastair        Lallie   Hilda   Ellie

*Mr Michie, auctioning a camera at a Camera Club meeting.*

*The Bught Mill, long since vanished, and the Diriebught Pool, both taken on glass plates by Alexander Dallas.*

*"Transport, Land, Passenger" is how this picture is filed in the Museum. The passenger has his "piece" firmly in his fist.*

*Rather more modern transport, and filed as "Social, people." Probably post-war children from the children's home.*

*Above: Floods at Ness Bank in 1892 before the building of Ness Bank Church (1902). Below left: Welcome supplies to a flood-bound house on Ness Bank, the church is just beyond. Below right: When cars fail, the horse comes into his own, on Ness Bank again below the church, Jock Clunas driving.*

*Summer in Inverness, bathers, paddlers and onlookers downstream of the Greig Street Suspension Bridge.*

181

*... in the winter of 1895. It is very unusual for the firths to freeze.* **182**

**183**

*A wedding group in Queensgate, before 1914. The minister is the Reverend Donald Macleod, minister of the Old High Church.*

**184**

*The unveiling of Flora Macdonald's statue on 26 July, 1899. She is looking up the Great Glen and the statue is unusual in having a dog beside the figure.*

185

Lord Baden Powell, the Founder of Scouting, came to Inverness to inspect the activities of the Highland Scouts in 1911. They put on a fine display in the Northern Meeting Park. B-P is easily distinguished in his Scout's hat and knee-breeches. The Press, with "light-weight" cameras, is much in evidence.

186

*Union Street decorated for Queen Victoria's Diamond Jubilee. At the end can be seen the old Caledonian Hotel.*

187

188

*Another Occasion. The Canadian Pipe Band marching across the mouth of Castle Street towards the river during the World Pipe Band Championships in 1966.*

The supporters of the Burgh's Coat of Arms, the elephant and the camel, have decided to support a lampstandard outside the Chapel yard. The circus was advertising its last performance, probably on the Bught Park.

189

190

Pomp in the High Street. The rider in the foreground is Chief Constable Macdonald. There is a pipe band, and a halberdier on the box of the first two carriages, so the Burgh is perhaps entertaining a "high heid yin."

*Queen Elizabeth the Queen Mother arriving at the Town House to be greeted by Provost Grigor on 6 August, 1953, when she was given the Freedom of the Burgh on the same day as the Queen's Own Cameron Highlanders. Lord Macdonald, the Lord Lieutenant of Inverness-shire, is between the Queen Mother and the Provost.*

*The platform is guarded by the Halberdiers, Colin Thomson being on the right. On the platform, the Queen Mother is talking to Major General Douglas Wimberley, Colonel of the Regiment, Lieutenant-General Sir Colin Barber, G.O.C. in C. Scottish Command, Lord Macdonald, Baillie William "Bobo" Mackay (Provost 1964-67) and Baillie Christie are behind them.*

191

192

*On the left, Mr James F. Campbell, with Mr A. Cameron, architect.*

193

194

*A 1945 group of Inverness County Councillors and officials who flew to Barra in "Canute" on the last time that Captain E. E. Fresson was the pilot. Left to right, Mr Carnegie (County Roads Surveyor), Lochiel, Hon. Alistair Fraser, Mr McKillop (County Clerk), Lord Macdonald and Mr Francis Walker.*

*Captain Fresson is seen receiving the Air Mail Pennant from Sir Frederick Williamson, Director of Postal Services. This marked the first Air Mail in the U.K. to be carried at ordinary Letter Rate. The date was 29 May, 1934 — Oakapple Day. Captain Fresson, of Highland Airways, flew the plane from the Longman Airfield to Orkney.*

*The Highland Strathspey and Reel Society in the 1920s.*

*The Strathspey and Reel Orchestra.*

*Standing: Mr Wheatley; ———; Mr Tom Gordon (Engine Driver); Mr Willie Mackay; Mr Duncan Grant (Watchmaker); Mr George Bell (Butcher); Mr Jim Macbean (Culcabock); Mr D.W. Call (Burgh Assessor for nearly 50 years). Sitting: Mr Alex Grant (Leader of the Society); Mr Duncan Mackenzie; Mr John Fraser; Mr Donald Riddell (Present Leader of the Society, 1978).*

*A group at the Strathspey and Reel Dinner. Back Row: Mr William Treasurer (Fire Master); Mr A. Duffie; Mr James Mackenzie; ———. Front Row: Mr Tom Macpherson; Mr John Fraser; Mr D.W. Call; Mr Alex. Grant.*

*A group at the Strathspey and Reel Dinner.*

*The Northern Amateur Operatic Society in "The Pirates of Penzance", 7th February, 1904.*

198

199

*Caley Ladies F.C.
26ᵗ May 1926.*

*The Caley Ladies Football Club in 1926. They continued until at least 1938 and presumably there were other teams for them to play.*

*Hockey Select Team. Second from left in the back row is Evan Barron, of the Inverness Courier. He was a referee and an international selector, and his powerful advocacy of Highland players brought the first, of many, Scottish "caps" to the North. He was also interested in cricket and was a founder of the Highland Rugby Club.*

200

201

*The Caledonian Football Club, 1922-23 with their trophies won that season.*

*Citadel F.C. 1928-29, North of Scotland Cup Champions. Back row, J. Mackenzie, W. Mackintosh (Trainer), K. Allan, W. Mackay, W. Sutherland, T. Brindle, J. Shaw (Captain), R. Reid (Vice-Capt.), R. Ogg (President), D. Forbes. Front Row, R. Logie, J. Cumming, G. Maciver, W. Munro, J. Paterson.*

**202**

*Agricultural Show about 1922. Left to right, Mr D. Gray (gunsmith), Miss Grace Ross, Miss E. M. Henderson, Mr G. Ross, Mr S. Cranston, Mr Angus McColl.*

**203**

*Early players of the Highland Rugby Club.*

*Nairn MacEwan is carried shoulder high by his admirers in 1976.*

**206**

**208**

*MacGillivray Senior League Final at the Bught Park, 2nd May, 1970. Above left: Willie Macbean (Newtonmore, stripes) and Jock Urquhart (Lovat) tussle for the ball, with Jackie Henton (Lovat keeper) on the alert. Above right: Camans raised at the Throw-up. Below: John Fraser (left) shoots one of his 4 goals. Brian Stewart (Newtonmore) and Jackie Henton (Lovat keeper). This was Newtonmore's 13th win of the Mac-Gillivray Senior League. Result, Lovat 2, Newtonmore 4.*

**207**

*A Shooting party at Dochfour. Left to right, Mackintosh of Mackintosh, Major the Hon. Alastair Fraser, Captain the Hon. Arthur Baillie, a son of Lady Burton, Lady Burton, Colonel J. E. B. Baillie, Lieut. Colonel O. S. Lloyd, Captain Burton Mackenzie, Lady Sybil Fraser and Mr Peter Laycock.*

209

210

*A successful stalk.*

*A Bonspiel in January, 1914. Mr A. N Macaulay, the Duke of Sutherland's solicitor from Golspie, on the left, is giving his instructions. The rival skip is John Birnie, Balnafettack, Provost of Inverness, and owner of the Glen Mor and Glen Albyn distilleries. The photo is by James Barron, junior, father of Miss Eveline Barron of the Inverness Courier.*

211

*The opening of the Longman Golf Course in about 1920.*

212

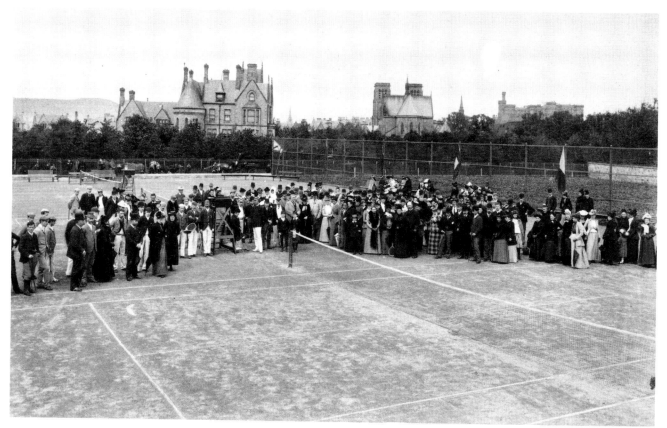

*The opening of the New Tennis Courts in Bishop's Road, 4 June, 1892.*

**213**

## EXTRAORDINARY NOVELTY AND ATTRACTION!
### *FOURTH APPEARANCE OF THE WONDER OF THE WORLD !!!*

# Mons. GOUFFE,
## CONTORTIONIST AND MAN-MONKEY,
WHOSE INDESCRIBABLE PERFORMANCES MUST BE WITNESSED TO BE BELIEVED.

*This present Evening, Friday, July 15, 1842,*

Will be represented Shakspeare's sublime Tragedy of

# MACBETH,
## KING OF SCOTLAND.

Embracing all Matthew Locke's celebrated Music, and produced with all the necessary Scenery, Costume, &c.

Macbeth (King of Scotland).............Mr CATHCART.
Duncan (King of Scotland)—Mr CLIFTON.   Malcolm (Prince of the Blood)—Mr DICKINSON.
Macduff  }  Generals in the Scottish Army.  }  Mr ROGERS.
Banquo  }                 }  Mr MARK.
The Bleeding Captain—Mr THOMPSON.   Rosse—Mr GILFILLAN.   Lennox—Mr SMITH.   Seyton—Mr RODs. RYDER.
Fleance—Master RYDER.   First Officer—Mr JONES.   Second Officer—Mr FLEMING.
Lady Macbeth .......Mrs RYDER.   Gentlewoman........Miss COWELL.
Hecate—Mr GILFILLAN.   First Speaking Witch—Mr WATKINS.   Second Speaking Witch—Mr ROGERS.
Third Speaking Witch—Mrs CLIFTON.   First Singing Witch—Miss J. DALY.   Second Singing Witch—Mrs THOMPSON.
Third Singing Witch—Miss COWELL.   Witches, Apparitions &c. by Supernumeraries.

*Programme of Principal Incidents in the Tragedy :—*

**MEETING OF MACBETH AND WITCHES ON THE BLASTED HEATH.**
EXTERIOR VIEW OF INVERNESS CASTLE IN THE OLDEN TIME—Painted expressly for the occasion.
**MURDER OF DUNCAN, KING OF SCOTLAND.**
"We should rejoice when good Kings bleed."
**CORONATION BANQUET IN THE CASTLE OF FORRES—AWFUL INCANTATION IN THE PIT OF ACHERON.**
"Show his eyes and grieve his heart,   |   Come-like shadows so depart."
**TERRIFIC ENCOUNTER BETWEEN MACBETH AND MACDUFF.**
PREDICTION FULFILLED—AWFUL OVERTHROW AND DEATH OF THE TYRANT.

End of the Tragedy,

## A COMIC MEDLEY DANCE BY MR THOMPSON.
## A COMIC SONG BY MR WATKINS.

To conclude with the popular Drama, written expressly for the wonderful display of Mons. GOUFFE'S peculiar talents, entitled

# THE BRAZILIAN APE.

# MAN-              MONKEY.

Captain Falconer (Governor of the Island)—Mr GILFILLAN.   Julian (his Son)—Master EDWIN RYDER.
Gustavus Marco Dunderhead (his Overseer)—Mr MARK.   Fabrioletto Dunderhead (his Son)—Mr WATKINS.   Harry Bluff (a Sailor)—Mr SMITH.
Zinga (a Slave)—Mr RODs. RYDER.   Bluenose—Mr THOMPSON.
**The Part of Jocko (the Island Ape) by Mons. GOUFFE.**
Overseers, Planters, Slaves, &c. by Supernumeraries.
Lauretta (the Governor's Ward)—Mrs ROGERS.   Mysa (an Indian Girl)—Miss COWELL.   Isabella Falconer—Mrs THOMPSON.

*Programme of the different Incidents in the Drama:—*

Governor's House in India—Interruption of Sports—Marco's charge—Artful plan to secure a bride for his Son—Lauretta's Inquiries—the Retort—The Governor's directions—
**GROTESQUE APPEARANCE OF THE BRAZILIAN APE.**
Mysa's Meeting with Lauretta—Production of the Bird of Paradise—Arrangements to receive Fabrioletto—His Arrival—Music charms the soul—Flights o Fancy—
Lauretta's promised introduction to the Monkey who has seen the world—March of Intellect—Fabrioletto's adventures in the wrong box—The Mistake.
MONSIEUR GOUFFE'S WONDERFUL FEATS ON THE
**BAMBOO TREE AND THE ROPE,**
CONCLUDING WITH HANGING HIMSELF BY THE NECK !!!
*(A feat that is acknowledged to surpass anything ever attempted in this Kingdom.)*
Fabrioletto on his Wanderings—His dislike of his Father's Treatment—His affection for the lovely Mysa—Her Generosity—Cupboard Love—Many a slip 'twixt the cup and the lip—
Rocks near the Sea Coast—Interview between the Governor and Lauretta—Her grateful acknowledgements—Sudden interruption—
**DREADFUL FATE OF THE VESSEL AND DEATH OF JOCKO.**

To-morrow (Saturday) will be represented ROB ROY, with the MONKEY and his DOUBLE, in which Mons. GOUFFE will perform,

### VIVANT REGINA ET PRINCEPS !

[Printed at the Courier Office, Inverness.]

*A Play Bill for Friday, July 15, 1842.*

*Harvesting in Fraser Park, Kingsmills Road, in 1926.*

215

216

*Firing the kilns at the Glen Albyn Distillery with peat and coke before 1950.*

*Filling barrels with whisky at the Glen Albyn Distillery, by the Muirtown Basin. Used for blending, the output in 1973 was 320,000 gallons a year.*

*Barrels lying in the lower vaults of Queen Mary's House. They will have been rolled down the slope in the foreground. Some of these vaults were removed when the house was demolished in the 1960s, and have been rebuilt, though turned through a right angle, in the entry hall of the Highlands and Islands Development Board building in Bank Street, where they may be seen.*

The funeral of Pipe Major John Macdonald leaving 3 Perceval Road for Kenneth Street in 1953. He was a Gold Medallist in 1890, and was later a King's Piper. Leading is Pipe Major Robert U. Brown, Queen's Piper.

**219**

**220**

The mourners include Pipe Major Macdonald's brother Andrew, and many famous pipers including John Macfadyen, William Ross and Hugh Macrae.

221

222

*Pauper's Coffin, Old High Church. This coffin has a loose lid and so can be used again and again as often as required, thus saving the parish funds the expense of a separate coffin for everyone who could not afford a better funeral.*

# SUBSCRIBERS

Mr J.A. Aitken.
Mrs M.F. Aitken.
Mr J. Alexander.
*Mrs Mary Alexander.
Mrs D.M. Allan.
Mr and Mrs E.T. Allan.
Mr Ian C.W. Allan.
Mr William Allan.
Mr George Anderson.
*Mr and Mrs Ian Anderson.
Mr Calum Anton.
Mr A.H. Archibald.
*Mr Richard Ardern.
Mrs Marie Atherton.
Mr and Mrs J.A.F. Bain.
*Miss Janet Banks.
Mr J.A. Barbour.
*Dr F.C. Barlow.
Mr G.M. Barnett.
*Miss E. Barron, O.B.E.
*Mrs M. Barron.
Mr James Barton.
Mr D.C. Bell.
*Miss Valerie Bell.
The Revd. S.J.G. Bennie.
Mr Angus W. Bethune.
Mrs C.A. Bisset.
*Miss J.M. Bithell.
Mr Alan Black.
Mr W.J. Bosworth.
Mr George Boyd.
Mr R.Y. Brace.
Mrs Alexandra Braid.
Mr Gordon M. Brown.
Mr James L. Brown.
Mr Fraser F. Bruce.
*Dr James Bruce.
*Mrs Douglas Bulloch.
Miss Esther F.A. Butchart.
Dr the Hon. Mrs Godfrey Butler.
*Mr S.W. Butler.
*Mr J.B. Caird.
Lt. Colonel A.E. Cameron.
Miss Eliz. C. Cameron.
Mrs F.M. Cameron.
Mr and Mrs James M. Cameron.
Mrs A.M. Campbell.
Mr Alexander Campbell.
Dr D.M. Campbell.
Miss E. Campbell.
*Miss E.M. Campbell.
*Mr James Campbell.

Miss J.M. Campbell.
Dr R.M. Campbell.
Mr T.W. Cane.
Mr Kenneth G. Cantlay.
Mr John R. Capp.
Mr Iain R. Cathcart.
Mrs Margaret E. Cathcart.
Mr F.M. Chester.
Mrs J.A. Chisholm.
*Miss M.L. Chisholm.
Mrs Nina Chisholm.
Mrs Sheila Chisholm.
Mr H.J. Chitty
Mr A.C. Christie.
Mr C.J. Claridge.
Miss Mhairi Clark.
*Mrs J.R. Clark.
Miss Mary B. Clyne.
*Mr Donald E. Coghill.
Mr and Mrs W.H. Cooper.
Mr R.J. Copland.
*Mr William Cran.
Mr and Mrs P. Crowe.
Mr John Cumming.
Mr and Mrs M. Cumming.
*Mr Andrew Currie.
Mr A. Connell Currie.
Miss Alison H. Curry.
Mr T.D. Curtis.
Miss I. Dallas.
Mr A.M. Davis.
*Mr and Mrs K.T. Davidson.
Miss Nora Davidson.
Mr W. Davidson.
Mr R. Dennis.
Mrs A. Dent.
Mr and Mrs L. Donald.
Mrs Wilde Donald.
*Mrs Dorothy Dow.
Mr M. Dow.
Mrs J. Easson.
Mr and Mrs S. Edmond.
Mrs M. Edwards.
Mrs P.C. Ellistone.
Mrs G.S. Elmslie.
Mr R. Emburey.
*Mr Eric C. England-Kerr.
*Mrs J.F. Eunson.
Mr David W. Evans.
Miss J. Fairgrieve.
Mr James Falconer.
*Mr and Mrs G. Farnell.

Mrs K.L. Farquharson.
Miss M.A. Ferguson.
Mrs S. Ferguson.
Mr B.W. Fieldsend.
Mr W.Y. Findlay.
Mrs A. Finlay.
*Mrs A.D. Forbes.
Mr C.S. Forbes.
*Miss M.E. Forrest-Sutherland.
Mr Alan C. Forsyth.
Mr G.G. Foubister.
Mr A. Fraser.
*Mr Alex Fraser.
*Miss Ann Fraser.
*Miss Catherine Fraser.
*Mrs Diana M. Fraser.
*Mr Donnie Fraser.
Mr Ian R. Fraser.
*Miss M. Fraser.
Mr William Fraser.
Mr W.J. Fraser.
Mr R.H.H. Furze.
Mrs J. Futcher.
*Mr and Mrs Gallacher.
Mrs A. Galloway.
Miss Margaret Gibson.
*Miss Anne Gillies.
*Mr William Glashan.
*Mrs J.A. Glynne-Percy.
Mr James Gordon.
Brigadier E.H.G. Grant.
Mrs Faith Grant.
*Miss Isabella M. Grant.
*Miss M. Grant.
Dr P.W. Grant.
Mr S.R. Grant.
Mr T.A.A. Grant.
*Dr Brenda Gray.
Miss C.M. Green.
Mrs A.J. Gunn.
Dr M.D.M. Hadley.
Dr Monty Hadley.
Mrs E.M. Hall.
Mr William Hamilton.
Miss Sheila M. Hanley.
Miss Vivian B. Hanley.
Dr W.P. Hanley.
Mr A.W. Harper.
Miss C.M. Harper.
Mr Gordon L. Harvey.
Mr Takeshi Hashiuchi.
Miss N.K. Hassan.

*Mr R. Hastie.
Mr David J.M. Hay.
Mrs Ishbel J. Hay.
Mr Alan C. Henderson.
Mr A.R. Henderson.
Mr D.M. Henderson.
*Mr and Mrs J.H.G. Herrick.
Mrs Hilda Hesling.
Mr John R. Hill.
Colonel Stanley Hill.
*Miss F.R. Horne.
Mr E. Hossack.
Mr Robert P. Hunter.
*Miss E.M. Hutton.
Mr Alan Gordon Imlah.
Mr P.C.P. Inglis.
Mr D.F. Ingram.
Mr G. Jenkins.
Mr John Jessiman.
Mrs and Mrs Tudor John.
Mr L.R. Johnston.
Mr James H. Johnstone.
Mr and Mrs John Johnstone.
Miss Moira Johnstone.
Mr W.M. Johnstone.
Mr H.R. Joyce.
Mrs J.M. Joyce.
*Mr Neil Kay.
Mr J. Keay.
Mr Patrick M.E. Kelsey.
Mr S.M. Kennedy.
*Lt. Col. and Mrs L.J.E. Kewley.
Mrs A.S. King.
*Mrs Renate Krebs.
Mr D.W. Kyte.
*Mr Alan B. Lawson.
Mr J.H. Lee.
Mr Gordon Leys.
Mrs Marion Lindsay.
Mr B. Lipton.
Mr W.E. Livingston.
Miss Marie Livingstone.
Mr A. Bryan G. Longmore.
Mr J. Andrew C. Luke.
Mr J.G. Lumsden.
*Dr Robert F. Macadam.
*Mrs Catriona Macarthur.
Mr R.A. McAvoy.
Mr M.W. McAvoy.
Mr D. Macbeath.
*Miss C.F. Macdonald.
Miss C.M. Macdonald.
*Dr D.J. Macdonald.
Mr D.W. Macdonald.
*Miss E. Macdonald.
Mrs Elizabeth MacDonald.

Mrs F. MacDonald.
*Mr H. MacDonald.
Mr Hector MacDonald.
Mr Hector A.M. Macdonald.
Mr Hugh S. Macdonald, O.B.E.
Mrs I. MacDonald.
Mr Ian A. MacDonald.
Mr and Mrs J. MacDonald.
Mrs Jean T. Macdonald.
Mr John A. Macdonald.
Mr and Mrs M. MacDonald.
Mr Murray MacDonald.
*Mrs N.A. Macdonald.
Mr R. Macdonald.
Mr R. Macdonald.
*Mrs W. MacDonald.
Miss J. MacDonell.
*Mr H.R. Macdougall.
Mr N.M.S. Macdougall.
Mr G.K.M. Macfarlane.
Mrs E. MacGregor.
Mr J.C. MacGregor.
Mr B. Macgruer.
Mrs J.E.K. MacGibbon.
Mrs Ishbel McGillivray.
Mrs C. Mackay.
Mr D.A. MacKay.
*Mr I.R. Mackay.
*Mrs Jessie Mackay.
*Miss T. Mackay.
*Mrs M.A.C. Mackell.
Mr B.F. MacKenzie.
*Miss C.A. Mackenzie.
Mrs D. Mackenzie.
Mr David G.C. Mackenzie.
Mr David J. Mackenzie.
Mr Donald I. Mackenzie.
Miss G. Mackenzie.
Mr H.F. Mackenzie.
Miss H.M. Mackenzie.
Mr J.S. Mackenzie.
Mrs K. Mackenzie.
Mr and Mrs Kenneth MacKenzie.
*Miss M. Mackenzie.
Mrs M. MacKenzie.
Miss Mhairi Mackenzie.
Mr Norman Mackenzie.
Miss P.A. Mackenzie.
Mr Peter A. Mackenzie.
*Miss Rhoda T. MacKenzie.
Mr S. Mackenzie.
Mrs T.L. Mackenzie.
Mrs Wilma M. MacKenzie.
Mr W. Mackenzie.
Mr Ian McKinlay.
Mr Donald J. Macinnes.

Mrs A. MacKinnon.
*Mrs J. MacKinnon.
*Mrs A.D. McIntosh.
*Mr J.W. MacKintosh.
Mrs M. Mackintosh.
Mrs Sarah Mackintosh.
Miss Anne L. Macintyre.
Mrs J. Macintyre.
Dr and Mrs John Macintyre.
Miss M. MacIntyre.
Mr Rob McIntyre.
Mr William John McIntyre.
Mr David O. Maclagan
   Wedderburn.
Mr A.O. Maclaren.
*The Revd. Allan Maclean of
   Dochgarroch.
*The Revd. Donald and Mrs
   Maclean of Dochgarroch.
*Miss Isobel McLean.
Mr G. Maclean.
Mrs G.L. MacLean.
*Miss M. MacLean.
Mr Ronald D. Maclean.
Mr and Mrs David I. MacLennan.
Mr D.E. MacLennan.
Mr and Mrs D.J. MacLennan.
Mr Duncan MacLennan.
Mrs K.M. MacLennan.
Mr R. Maclennan.
Mr Robert McLennan.
*Miss Christina M. Macleod.
Miss M.E. Deirdre MacLeod.
*Mr and Mrs J. Macleod.
Mr and Mrs J.M. Macleod.
Miss Jean M. Macleod.
Mr R.J. Macleod.
Mr I. Torquil Macleod.
*Miss E. Macmillan.
Mrs M. Macmillan.
Mr I. MacNeil.
Miss Anne M. MacPherson.
*Dr Ian Macpherson.
Miss M. Macpherson.
*Mrs I. MacQueen.
Mr and Mrs D. MacRae.
Mr R.J. McRae.
*Group Captain Molly Macrae.
Mrs M.H. Main.
Mrs Shona Ruth Malcolm.
Mr and Mrs Albert Mann.
Miss E.M. Manson, M.A.
*Miss E.B. Martin.
Mr C.M. Masson.
*Miss A.J. Matheson.
*Miss C.M. Matheson.

Mr Donald Matheson.
Mr Donald F. Matheson.
Mr J.G. Matheson.
*Mr H.A. Maxwell, O.B.E.
*Mr J.R. Mayne.
*Mr and Mrs Edward Meldrum.
Mr A.C. Mellor.
*Mr J.A. Menzies.
Mr and Mrs A.D. Merchant.
Mr and Mrs B.A. Merchant.
Mr and Mrs A. Mills.
Millburn Academy.
Mr K.R. Minford.
*Mrs Helen Morrison.
Mr J. Morrison.
*Mrs Jessie Morrison.
Mr William Morrison.
Mrs E. Morton.
Mr R. Mulholland.
Mr D.R. Munro.
*Miss Ellen R. Munro.
Mrs I.H. Munro.
*Dr J.G. Munro.
Mrs M. Munro.
Thos. Munro and Co.
Mr F.J. Murchison.
*Mrs D.G. Murray.
Miss H.M. Murray.
Mr Neil W. Murray.
*Mr John Musker.
*Mrs T. Nesbitt.
Mr P.J. Nicholson.
Miss Margaret Hillier Orme.
Mr William George Panton.
Mr Clifford F. Parr.
Mrs P. Patience.
Mr John Paton.
Miss S.D. Phillips.
Mr S.H. Pickett.
Mr A.G. Pollitt.
Mr J.M. Pottie.
Mr K.R. Povey.
Mr C. Quinn.
Mrs Christina Rattray.
*Mr Martin Regan.

Mr D. Reid.
Mr John C. Reid.
Miss M.J. Reid.
Mrs J.M. Rhind.
*Mrs Catherine A. Richards.
Mr G.D. Richardson.
*Miss F. Riddle.
*Dr Robert Rines.
Mr A.J. Robertson.
Miss Catriona Robertson.
Mr N.D. Robertson.
*Sheriff S. Scott Robinson.
Mr James Rose.
Mr D.F. Ross.
Miss Fiona Ross.
Mrs M.A. Ross.
Mrs Mary Ross.
Mr W. Ross.
Mr and Mrs J.L. Roy.
Mr M.F. Sangster.
*Mr L.F. Sarjeant.
Mr J.M. Scott.
The Right Revd. George Sessford.
Dr M.F. Shanks.
Mrs Joan Sharp.
Mr W.N. Sharp.
Major C.J. Shaw of Tordarroch.
*Miss K. Sinclair.
Mr L.A. Skinner.
*Mrs Jean Slesser.
Mr J.H. Smart.
Mrs Anne Smith.
Dr Anthony D. Smith.
Mrs J.E.K. Smith, M.A.
Mr and Mrs D.G. Smith.
*Mrs E.M. Smith.
Mr Ranald M. Smith.
Mr David G. Somerville.
Mr F.D.N. Spaven.
Mrs M.E. Squires.
Mr Alexander Stewart.
*Mrs Katharine Stewart.
Mr Robin Stewart.
The Revd. Donald Strachan.
Mr Harry Strachan.

Mr Douglas Stuart.
Miss M.M. Sutherland.
Mrs M.B. Taylor.
Mr P.G. Taylor.
Mr M.S. Taylor.
*Mr Wilfred Taylor.
*Mrs A.M. Tedcastle.
Mr Geoffrey Thomson.
Mrs J. Thomson.
*Miss J.E. Thomson.
Mrs John Thomson.
Mr Leslie D. Thomson.
Miss Helen A. Thorne.
Mr George Totten.
Mrs F.I. Tough.
Miss H.E. Tough.
*Miss Helen E. Urquhart.
Mr K.G. Urquhart.
Miss Angela G. Veitch.
Mrs Margaret M. Veitch.
Miss Patricia M. Veitch.
Mr Alan Watson.
Mr William T. Weatherspoon.
Mrs Jean E. Weir.
*Mr Alexander Whyte.
*Miss M.F. Whyte.
Mr H.W. Wilkinson.
*Miss C. Williams.
*Mr E. Williams.
Dr Frank Williams.
Mr Allan S. Wilson.
Mr D.C.R. Wilson.
Mr D.G. Wilson.
Mr James I. Wilson.
Mr John P.I. Wilson.
*Mrs N.B. Wilson.
Mr M.J. Wilton
Mr William Wishart.
Mr Iain M. Wotherspoon.
Mr Evan D. Wylie.
Mrs R. Young.
Mr R.C. Young.
*Mr R.D.M. Young.